COW

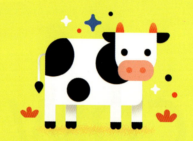

COW

.＿

boil

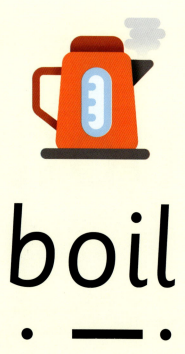

boil

• — •

beard

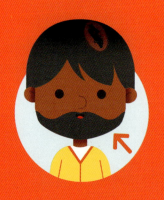

beard

• —— •

hair

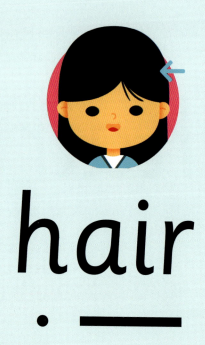

hair

•   —

cure

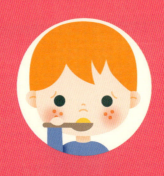

cure

ladder

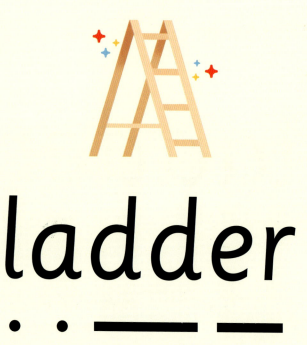

ladder

• • — —

town

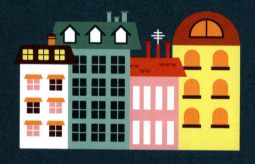

town

soil

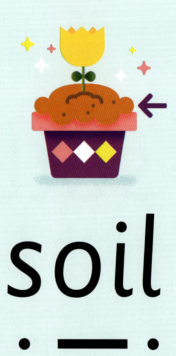

soil

•‒•

chair

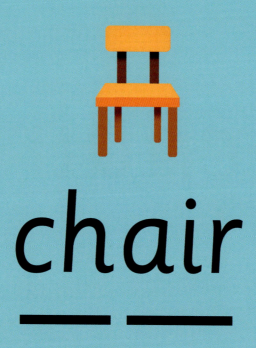

chair

___ ___

singer

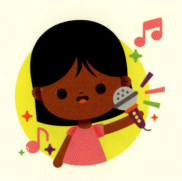

singer
· · __ __

They dig
the soil.

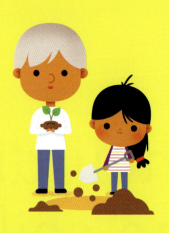

They dig
the soil.

They can hear
an owl.

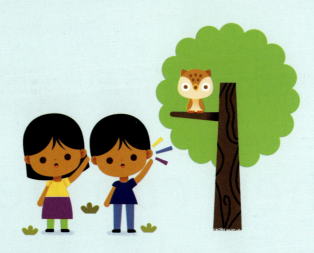

They can hear
an owl.